Adirondack Bear Tales

D.C. Gilbert

Copyright © 2018 Darren Curtiss Gilbert
All rights reserved. No part of this publication may be reproduced, stored in a retrieval system or transmitted, in any form or by any means, electronic, mechanical, photocopying, recording or otherwise, without permission of the author.
ISBN: 978-1-7908-1729-0

DEDICATION

I am dedicating this book to my mother, Ardis Eileen Gilbert, who lived her life on her terms and shared so many incredible adventures with her husband and sons.

ACKNOWLEDGMENTS

Thank you to Curtiss Gilbert, Daniel Gilbert, Carol Piser and Fred Klippel for sharing their recollections of these family stories and helping me keep them as accurate is possible.

Introduction

Growing up and spending summers at Raquette Lake in the Adirondack Park was a wonderful experience. From tenting at Golden Beach Campsite to staying at my grandparent's camps on Burketown Road or tenting on our lot while we built our camp in Burketown, I carry these beautiful memories with me every day.

If you spend much time in the Adirondacks at all, you soon learn about the black bears! There are plenty of them around. My first adventures involving black bears revolved around going to the Raquette Lake dump on Friday nights to watch them feed. Generations of bears had come to rely on local dumps as a reliable source of food. When the dumps were closed and replaced with bear-proof convenient centers, the bears had few alternatives other than to raid dumpsters and campgrounds. Encounters between humans and bears became more frequent as time passed. Mostly, the contacts were harmless. Occasionally they were not. And, when they were not, it often ended badly for the bears.

The stories in this collection are true tales of encounters between members of my family and bears over our years tenting and camping in the Adirondacks. They occurred in areas around Raquette Lake and Burketown. The core of each story is factual. Any "literary license" taken is only to improve the flow and readability of the story.

These stories are not long. The book is only about fifty pages. But I believe the stories are quite enjoyable. I hope you enjoy reading them as much as I enjoy remembering them.

D.C. Gilbert

A Night Time Stroll at Golden Beach

It was dark. When the lights go out in the Adirondacks, it gets very dark, even pitch black. In the tent, you literally couldn't see your hands in front of your face. The twelve-year-old girl whose name was Ardis squirmed in her sleeping bag. Her mother had warned her not to drink that last bottle of Coca-Cola before going to bed. But Ardis had not listened, and now she had to use the bathroom!

What time is it? She wondered. *Can I make it until morning?*

She did not think she could. Working quietly, trying not to awaken her parents or her older brother and younger sister, Ardis got herself ready. There was little chance of waking them since her father was loudly snoring away. All four slept blissfully and unaware. The cool Adirondack nights did make for some great sleeping.

Reaching for the flashlight she kept on the floor of the tent by her sleeping bag; the young girl turned it on. Being careful not to shine the light in anyone's face, Ardis unzipped the zipper on the side of her sleeping bag and crawled out.

First, she put on her plaid flannel shirt because the night air was quite chilly once she was out of her warm sleeping bag. Next, she reached for the beaded leather moccasins her mother had bought for her on yesterday's trip into the town of Inlet. Her mother especially loved to shop in Mary's Gift Shop. Her older brother, Ken, and her younger sister, Carol, had gotten moccasins as well. Ken would have preferred a bow and arrow.

Making her way to the front flap of the big cabin tent, she unzipped the mosquito netting at the front, stepped out, and zipping the netting back, made her way down the path toward the closest women's bathroom. It was a short walk, maybe fifty yards. Golden Beach Campground had several men's and women's bathrooms and shower houses strategically located throughout the campground.

Ardis made her way along the path, the beam of the flashlight projecting its stream of light on the ground a few feet in front of her. She was about halfway there when she froze. Clearly defined in the circle of light from the flashlight were two large black paws. The paws were attached to two somewhat furry black legs. Not panicking, the young girl tilted her light ever-so-slightly upward. Standing in the path a few feet in front of her, clearly framed in the beam of her flashlight, was a rather large black bear!

Carefully, the girl lowered the light again until only the bear's paws were visible. She slowly began to back up one step at a time while keeping the bear's two paws in the circle of light. Ardis wanted to be able to see if the bear moved toward her. When the beam of light could no longer reach the bear's paws, she turned and made her way swiftly back to the tent. Quickly unzipping the mosquito netting, Ardis stepped inside and zipped it shut. In a few minutes, she was back in her sleeping bag, listening to her father snore.

Ardis decided she could wait until the morning to use the bathroom after all!

A Night in the Nash Rambler

The 1956 Nash Rambler pulled into a campsite at the Golden Beach Campground on Raquette Lake in Upstate New York. A young man got out from the driver's side and opened the passenger door for his very pregnant wife. It felt good to stretch their legs. They had just completed the four-hour drive to Raquette Lake from North Adams, Massachusetts.

The expectant mother's parents, Erwin and Eileen Klippel, had arrived at Golden Beach the weekend before and set up camp. They were staying at the campground for two weeks as was their summer custom. In earlier years when their first two children, Ken and Ardis, were younger, they'd camped at the Eighth Lake Campground. By the time Carol arrived on the scene, they'd tried Golden Beach and discovered they liked it much better. Eileen loved the beautiful golden sand for which the beach got its name and was quite content to sit out on the beach with a good book for hours reading.

Over the years, Erwin and Eileen had become quite expert at camping in the Adirondacks. The cabin tent was set up under a tarp for added protection against the often-heavy north woods rains. Erwin always dug a trench around the tent to drain the rainwater away, sending it downhill towards the lake. The ditch kept the floor of the tent nice and dry during the heaviest of rains.

There was a dining-tarp over the picnic table with the Coleman gas stove and kitchen box positioned at one end. The ice box with the perishable food items sat along the side of the tent in the cool shade of the tent's rain tarp. There were four folding lawn chairs in a half circle around the fireplace in anticipation of the campfire and conversation that would undoubtedly occur later that evening. It was a very comfortable and happy campsite.

When the Rambler pulled in at the site, it was early evening. Erwin and Eileen got up from the game of Rummy they were playing and went to greet the young couple. After hugs all around, Eileen led her daughter to one of the lawn chairs and made her comfortable.

Erwin led his son-in-law, Curt, on a tour of the campsite. The young man, an engineer by profession, was impressed with the setup; especially the trenching system to drain off the rainwater. It was quite a professional looking job.

Erwin busied himself with the fireplace, and soon the campfire was merrily crackling away as the four caught up on everything that occurred since their last visit. The baby was due in early July, just a few short weeks away. Eileen fussed over her daughter, making sure she was taking good care of herself. Ardis assured her mother that she was. She was, after all, a registered nurse. The young couple laughed as they described their new apartment in North Adams. They had moved there when Curt was offered his first job as a chemical engineer. It was a third-story attic apartment, and Ardis joked that the bathroom was so small you could sit on the toilet and soak your feet in the tub at the same time. They were certainly going to have to find something a bit bigger once the baby arrived.

It was a pleasant evening, and as is so often the case when having a such a great time, the time flew by quickly. It was soon late and all four were ready for bed.

Erwin excused himself and went to prepare the icebox for the night. There are a good number of black bears in the Adirondacks. Therefore, every night Erwin suspended the icebox out of bear reach between two nearby trees by attaching a rope to its handles. Curt offered to help, but his father-in-law declined, saying he had his system down pat.

Instead, Curt went over to the old Nash Rambler. He and Ardis did not have a tent, so it was very convenient that the Rambler's front seat folded down to make a reasonably comfortable bed.

In short order, Erwin had the icebox secured, and good nights were said. Erwin and Eileen headed to their tent, and Curt made Ardis comfortable in the Rambler. It was soon quiet, with everyone settled in for the night. There is nothing like a peaceful night's sleep in the fresh north woods air.

Thump! Bash!
Ardis opened her eyes.
Bash! Bash! Thump!
What in the world is that, she wondered? Reaching over, Ardis shook her husband to wake him.
"What is it?" he asked.
"Listen," she replied.
Thump! Bash! Thump!
Curt sat up, bumping his head on the roof of the Rambler.
"What the hell is that?"
Curt crawled forward and retrieved his keys from the dash where he'd placed them the night before. Putting the ignition key in the switch, he turned it one click and reaching for the knob of the light switch, pulled it, turning the headlights on.

There, standing directly in the beam of the Nash Rambler's headlights was a huge black bear reared up on its hind legs. It was furiously batting at the icebox with its forepaws. While the icebox would have been out of reach for most bears, this was a pretty big fellow, and he wanted the icebox's contents in the worst way.

Bash! Thump. Thump! Bash!
With each swat, the icebox swung wildly on the ropes that were tied to its handles, suspending it between the trees. Curt thought it was incredible that the handles were still attached!

Suddenly they weren't, and the icebox tumbled to the ground. The bear pawed at the lid until it opened. Reaching in, the bear extracted a bunch of grapes. To Curt and Ardis's amazement, the bear sat down and plucked grapes from the bunch one at a time and popped them into his mouth continuing until they were all gone. The bear placed the now grapeless vines on the ground and turned his attention back to the icebox.

Curt was trying to decide what to do about the bear and finally tried beeping the Rambler's horn. The bear stopped and looked toward the car. After a second, the bear again turned his attention back to rummaging around in the icebox.

The young man laid into the horn again. This time holding it for an extended blast. After giving the Rambler an extremely disgusted look, the bear stopped and ambled off in search of another "quieter" food source. The campsite was still once more.

The next morning after the four had cooked and eaten breakfast, Ardis assisted her mother in doing the dishes and cleaning up. Erwin approached his son-in-law, Curt.

"That was good thinking last night. We weren't sure what to do. I thought about trying to chase the bear off, but they can be pretty unpredictable, and that was a pretty big fellow. So, I decided we were safer staying put in the tent and letting him have the food."

The younger man laughed. "It was the only thing I could think of to do. I'm glad it worked!"

"By the way," Erwin went on, "Do you want to take a drive into Old Forge with me? As a result of last night's excitement, we need a new icebox."

A Trip to the Dump

It's Friday evening in the Adirondacks. So, what do you do? What kind of entertainment venues were available to vacationers in the north woods? One of our family favorites was to go to the dump! Yep! I am serious. We would go to the dump to watch the bears. It was quite popular among those in the know. The bears would come out in the early evenings to feed on all the delightful morsels we humans would throw away.

The Raquette Lake Dump was located a mile or so down an old dirt road that headed out of Raquette Lake Village and into the wilderness. This road had initially been the rail bed for a private railroad line owned by the Vanderbilts. The Vanderbilt family built an Adirondack great camp, Camp Sagamore, near Raquette Lake. They and their guests would take a private train from Utica, New York up to Raquette Lake. There they would board a boat and steam across South Bay to head up the South Inlet. A mile or so up South Inlet, at the falls, where it became impassable for boats, they would board a stagecoach and travel along a road that ran past the Vanderbilt's power-house, then a small dam that controlled water to the old powerhouse, and finally to the smaller private lake from which South Inlet flows. This small lake was their destination. Camp Sagamore sat on its shores.

But I digress. This tale is supposed to be about bears and the Raquette Lake dump.

This particular Friday evening my brother, Dan, and I headed to the dump with our grandparents. They had an AMC Hornet, and we sat in the back. We turned down the old dirt road. Being an old railway bed, it was a pretty straight shot, and we soon approached the dump. There were already several black bears, an assortment of ages and sizes, out prowling around in the garbage bags looking for tasty tidbits.

My Grandfather pulled up pretty close because he had a bag of trash to add to the pile. Grandpa told us all to stay in the car. He would throw the garbage on the heap and then we would back up a bit to watch the bears. Grandpa got out and retrieved the bag from the trunk and started toward the piled-up bags of garbage. He wanted to get close enough to throw the bag onto the pile.

One mid-sized bear spotted our grandfather making his way toward the trash heap. The bear undoubtedly noticed that he was carrying a new bag of possible snacks. Naturally, the intrigued bear made his way toward our grandfather. Now, our grandfather was not a pushover. He was a big man, strong and stubborn. He'd decided that the bear was not getting the garbage until he threw it on the pile. The bear, however, having no idea of just who he was dealing with had other ideas, and that garbage bag quickly became a significant source of contention.

Grandpa saw the bear coming and yelled at it in an attempt to "bluff" the bear into backing off. However, as I stated earlier, the bear had no idea just who he was up against, so naturally, he kept coming. Soon the bear was between our grandfather and the trash heap. Grandpa took another step toward the bear and clutching the garbage bag tightly, yelled again. The bear, unimpressed, took another step toward our grandfather. And then, the bear took another step. Our grandfather, realizing that the bear was not intimidated, began backing toward the car with the bear following. The bear's coming toward the vehicle scared our grandmother who reached up and locked both car doors.

Grandpa backed up all the way to the car with the bear following him every step of the way. Keeping his eyes on the bear, he made his way to the driver-side door and reached down to open it. It was locked!

"Boots, unlock the door," he yelled. He called her "Boots" because of the black patent leather boots she was wearing when they first met. Eileen first started wearing boots in high school. We called her "Nanny," of course.

"Erwin, get rid of the garbage. Let the bear have it," Nanny yelled back. Grandpa was now circling the car with the bear following him. It was exciting for my brother and me sitting in the back seat.

"Boots, unlock the door!" he yelled again.

"Get rid of the garbage, Erwin" Nanny yelled back. Grandpa had, by now, circled the car several times with the bear in dogged pursuit. Finally realizing that something had to give, as he came around again to the front of the vehicle, Grandpa hurled the bag of garbage as hard as he could toward the heap of garbage bags about thirty yards away. Nanny reached over and unlocked the driver-side door and Grandpa, jerking the door open, slid into the seat and slammed the door closed. The bear, however, had already headed off in the direction Grandpa had hurled the bag and was now sniffing speculatively at it.

There was an uncomfortable moment of silence in the car. Finally, Grandpa spoke.

"For the love of Pete, Boots, why wouldn't you unlock the door."

"Erwin, I was not letting you in here with the garbage. What if the bear tried to get in here too!"

"Oh, for heaven sakes!" Grandpa retorted. The bear watching was cut short, and it was a hushed ride back to their camp at Burke Town.

Donny Trees a Bear

As I have already mentioned a few times, it gets dark early in the Adirondacks. The night's fire was about out with just a few glowing embers left in the cinder block fireplace. Two young boys, Darren and Dan, had already brushed their teeth and were quite ready for bed. They unzipped the mosquito netting and went into the large canvas cabin tent that sat on a wooden tent platform. Donny, a 35-lb Spanish Pointer, followed the two boys into the tent. Zipping the netting behind them, the tired boys crawled into their sleeping bags. They had air mattresses underneath the sleeping bags and were comfortably settled in for the night. Donny settled down between the two of them. Soon all three were sound asleep. Full days of endless adventures in the crisp Adirondack air made for good sleeping.

A little while later, Curt and Ardis entered the tent and prepared for bed. Their sleeping bags were laid out on canvas folding cots and had air mattresses laid under them as well. It was a reasonably comfortable arrangement. Soon all five were contentedly sleeping away.

Tomorrow would be another new and glorious day. Nanny and Grandpa were going to take their two grandsons fishing over in the northern part of Raquette Lake. They had a beautiful Thompson Chris-Craft boat which was often used for fishing, waterskiing, and general sightseeing excursions. With a little luck, they would have a good catch of fish for supper. Nanny, much to Grandpa's dismay, always seemed to catch a lot of fish with her little Popeil Pocket Fisherman. This fact really irritated Grandpa because he had only the "best" in fishing tackle and Nanny still caught more fish than him with her small plastic folding fishing pole!

Sometime during the night, Donny awoke and let out a terrible growl. The two boys and their parents instantly sat up in their sleeping bags.

What was that?

There was another growl from Donny, and like a flash, he was up. A second later he'd torn right through the mosquito netting and was off like a shot, snarling and growling like a wild animal protecting its young. Suddenly, there was another growl, and it wasn't Donny. Curt was now up with his flashlight, unzipping the mosquito netting to see what was going on while the rest of the family dug for their lights. Everyone kept a flashlight handy just in case. They could hear the dog barking wildly just a few yards from the tent.

A few seconds later all four flashlight beams were shining in the direction of the growling and snarling dog. Donny was at the base of an old rotten beech tree about 30 feet from the tent. He was growling and barking ferociously at something up in the tree. Raising the flashlight's beams a bit higher revealed a young black bear. The bear had scrambled up an old rotten tree trunk to get away from the crazy dog.

The tree and its bark were rotten enough that the bear's claws could not get a good grip. The bear would begin to slide down the tree, which would cause Donny to renew his barking and growling frenzy. This frenzied barking would, in turn, cause the bear to scramble a bit higher; only to start slipping again. If the bear had taken the time to look down to see the size of the dog that was barking at him, he might have been tempted to jump down and deal with the barking dog. Fortunately for Donny, the bear didn't decide to do this.

The barking, scrambling, and slipping went on for several minutes. Suddenly the bear completely lost its grip on the tree and tumbled to the ground. Rolling over, the bear jumped to its feet and took off into the dark north woods with Donny right behind him, barking and growling as he went. The boys and both parents called after Donny.

"Donny, Come! Donny, Come here!"

But it was no use. Donny was long gone, chasing after the black bear. Eventually, the two boys and their parents went back to bed. The boy's wondered if they would ever see their dog again.

Donny was not back the next morning when the boys left to go fishing with their grandparents. He was not back that afternoon when they got back from their fishing trip.

Then, later that evening, as the family sat down for a supper of Ravioli, bread and butter, and some of Ardis' homemade raspberry cobbler, Donny came trotting up to the picnic table with a delighted look on his face. It looked like he was grinning from ear to ear!

Donny was utterly covered with Adirondack marsh mud, bits of twigs, pine needles, and leaves. He was the hero of the day, having saved the cooler from being raided by the prowling black bear. And Donny, after his two-day-long adventure in the north woods, was also darn hungry!

Black Bears and Birds

What do black bears and birds have in common, you might ask? Well, let me tell you. Besides the fact that they both love birdseed, they had my uncle in common.

Klippels tend to be stubborn. My grandfather was stubborn, my mother was stubborn, her sister was stubborn, and my uncle, Kenneth Klippel, was stubborn. Now, that's a lot of stubbornness! Mostly, it was stubborn in a good way … the kind of stubbornness that allows one to stick to their guns and get things done.

Uncle Ken also enjoyed watching birds. Upon his retirement, he moved from Binghamton, NY to Raquette Lake where he settled into the camp he and my grandfather had built many years earlier. One of the first things he did was set up a bird feeder in the front yard. Nothing fancy. Just one of those shepherd's hook-type metal supports with a bird feeder hanging from it. That is when the problems began!

The first clue that this would become problematic was when he awoke early one morning to some strange noises on his screened-in front porch. Upon investigation, he discovered a young black bear had broken into his screen-in porch and was busily munching away on the giant bag of wild bird seed Uncle Ken had stored there. Luckily, he was able to shoo the bear away. Subsequently, he began keeping the bird seed in the old outhouse that he'd converted into a tool shed. Things seemed quiet after that, and the problem seemed to be solved. At least, until the next spring!

One evening, Uncle Ken returned from a fishing excursion with some of his buddies into the north part of Raquette Lake. He and a few friends had left early in the morning on a fishing expedition for lake trout. When they'd returned, Uncle Ken pulled in to park at his camp and noticed the bird-feeder support was pushed over, the bird feeder was pretty badly smashed up, and the bird seed was, of course, gone. Nonplussed, he merely went into Old Forge and got a stronger support and a new bird feeder. The next day, the new birder feeder was in place, and his happy little feathered friends were back. This last episode, however, was not the end of the story. Not by a long shot! The battle of the bird feeder quickly escalated and was waged throughout several years.

Several times the bird feeder was raided by a black bear and the bird seed eaten. Each time the bird feeder had to be replaced, and the mounting system became more substantial each time.

I still remember the year he'd tried to use a 4×4 post. Uncle Ken had dug a hole, set the 4×4 in it, and poured concrete around it for a strong base. I was staying at our camp for a week that summer and got the scoop. This time he saw the bear, and it was a big one. Ken was headed out for the day when he discovers the bear in his front yard. The bear simply snapped the 4×4 over and was busily munching down on the bird seed that had once been in the now mangled bird feeder.

Uncle Ken, angry now, went in to get his shotgun. The bear was gone when he returned. I guess the bear had decided that he'd overstayed his welcome. Uncle Ken later told me that he wasn't going to shoot the bear; he just wanted to scare it off. Later that afternoon, he headed back to Old Forge for more concrete and a steel pole. "Something like a basketball goal post," as Uncle Ken put it. When I headed back to Tennessee, he was out there digging an even bigger hole for the new "steel-pole" bird feeder's concrete base he was going to pour.

The next year I returned, only to notice that there was no bird feeder in sight. Intrigued, I continued up to our camp, unloaded my gear, and then walked down the road to Uncle Ken's camp to get, as Paul Harvey would say, "the rest of the story!" Uncle Ken was sitting out on his screened-in porch when I walked up. I asked about the "goal-post" bird feeder. Uncle Ken just shook his head, telling me that he'd returned from a trip to Warrensburg where he'd been visiting with a friend, only to find the metal post pushed over, the bird feeder demolished, and of course, the bird seed gone.

"The bear just pushed the damn thing over, pulling the concrete base right out of the ground," he explained.

"At least, the bear had to work for it," I observed, trying hard not to grin. I did know how stubborn my uncle was and how much he hated losing, especially to a bear. "Are you going to try again?" I asked.

Uncle Ken again shook his head. "Nope! If I keep this going, eventually I will end up having to shoot that damn bear … and I don't want to do that. Might upset the neighbors!" I nodded, understanding that under his gruff exterior, my uncle had a big heart and he didn't want to shoot that bear. Uncle Ken went on," I guess the only real losers here are my birds … but they'll be alright."

Aunt Betty Swats a Bear

Our camp sat near the end of Burketown Road near the Miller's old camp and Jack Camp's old place. Jack Camp, a permanent resident, was the local coroner and constable and kept an eye on things for those of us who owned summer camps in the area.

Across the road was a camp that belonged to my Great Uncle Wagner and Aunt Betty. Uncle Wagner was my Grandfather Klippel's older brother. My Nanny and Grandpa had a camp back down the road, closer to

Burke's Marina. I remember, as a young boy, helping cut the rafters for Uncle Wagner's camp when it was being built.

This particular evening several younger family members were sitting around the stone-encircled campfire in front of Uncle Wagner's camp. There was myself, my younger brother, three cousins who were all boys, and two other cousins who were both girls. We probably ranged in ages from 8 to 15. And, we were having a grand time toasting marshmallows on sticks we had cut earlier from a nearby Beech tree.

Uncle Wagner, Aunt Betty, Grandpa, and Nanny were sitting at the kitchen table in the camp playing Rummy 500. This card game was a favorite Adirondack evening pastime in our families. In addition, we also regularly enjoyed playing Pitch, Cribbage, and Pinochle. Family card games were a regular event. Tonight though, our parents were across the road in our camp spending a quiet evening reading. I guess they probably needed a break from my brother and me. We could sometimes be a handful!

It was funny how some of us liked to see the marshmallows blaze, preferring them charred on the outside and melted on the inside. I preferred mine golden brown on the outside and warm in the middle. Therefore, I would concentrate a bit harder than some on the task at hand, selecting just the right nest of red-hot coals, and turning the marshmallow constantly to get a beautiful even golden-brown color. I guess that is why I was the last one to notice that a black bear had come out of the woods, no doubt attracted by the enticing smell of burning marshmallows.

Aunt Betty was a short, stocky woman and not afraid of much that I can remember. I guess Aunt Betty must have heard the ruckus as we all started yelling and scattered to give the bear plenty of room because she exploded through the screen door of the camp armed with a straw broom. The black bear being young, maybe a little older than a yearling, did not know what he had unwittingly stumbled into. He just wanted marshmallows, but what he found was more like a stirred-up hornet's nest.

Wielded by Aunt Betty, the sweeping end of that broom attacked that poor bear from all angles at once, and Betty let loose with a barrage of "Shoos, Scrams, and Git's." The bear quickly decided the marshmallows were definitely not worth the trouble and took off just as fast as he could back into the woods letting loose with bawling sounds that were a cross between a bellow and a whine.

All us kids were safe and sound. But that incident ended any marshmallow toasting for the night as Aunt Betty herded us all into their camp. Our parents, alarmed at the sudden change in the sounds coming from across the road, had appeared just as the bawling bear disappeared into the dark woods and quickly escorted us back across the road. We were soon settled in for the night up in the loft. I don't think that bear ventured into our region of the Adirondack Park ever again.

The Demise of Old Three-toes

Three-toes was a grouchy, old bear. He was also large for a black bear. Folks around Burketown who occasionally spotted him estimated he might weigh between 450 and 500 pounds. This is relatively large for an Adirondack black bear. You knew when old three-toes was poking around from his distinctive tracks. His left fore-paw was missing the two outer toes, leading of course, to his nickname. Nobody knew how he'd lost those two front toes. Speculation was abundant. Maybe he'd lost them in a fight with another bear, or perhaps a near miss with some bear trap. Whatever the cause, it almost certainly contributed to his sour disposition.

A couple of camps down Burketown Road from my grandparent's camp and in the direction of Burke's Marina lived a friend of the family. A local contractor and handyman named Maurice, he'd built the camp belonging to my other grandparents on the lot next to ours near the end of the road.

As of late, old three-toes had become the frequent topic of discussion up and down the road. Folks spotted him on the prowl regularly, and he'd been getting in to some real mischief, causing damage to camps, screen windows, front porches, etc. So far nothing serious had occurred, but many felt it was merely a matter of time.

On this particular morning, Maurice got up early to go fishing. And, living alone, began cooking himself breakfast. He'd opened the front door to his camp to allow the cold, crisp morning air to pass through the screen door. Unfortunately, this also allowed the smell of cooking bacon to waft its way out through the screen door, where it was carried along on that same morning breeze. The tantalizing smell of frying bacon proved to be irresistible to old three-toes who happened to be passing by. The bear turned and followed the enticing aroma right up to Maurice's camp screen door.

Three-toes decided that the screen door was not going to keep him from getting to that delicious smelling bacon! Maurice heard the crashing sound of three-toes clawing right through the screen door. He turned in time to see the big bear coming down the short hallway toward his kitchen area. Maurice quickly retreated from the kitchen area and in the opposite direction. He made his way to his den where he kept a loaded 12-gauge shotgun on his rifle rack.

Maurice grabbed the 12-gauge and headed back to the kitchen where three-toes was making quite a mess of things. He yelled at the bear first, hoping to scare it off. He did not want to shoot the bear. Unfortunately, three-toes was having none of it. Old Three-toes figured this was now his bacon and, as far as that went, it was also now his kitchen. Maurice simply had no choice. Taking careful aim with the shotgun, he fired.

While many in the Burketown area were saddened by the death of three-toes, a lot of people slept a bit more soundly at night. It is an unfortunate thing when black bears lose their fear of people. It never turns out well for the bear.

I hope this story touches you and reminds you why it is so important not to feed the bears. While black bears can indeed be cute, they are still wild animals.

Campfire BBQ Chicken

It was another nice cool Adirondack evening. Therefore, Grandma Gilbert decided to make campfire BBQ chicken using the outside fireplace behind the camp. This way they could be outside to enjoy the fresh evening air. There would also be less mess to clean up in the kitchen after dinner.

Grandpa started a wood fire in the cinder block fireplace and kept feeding it seasoned beech wood. Soon, there was a nice bed of red-hot coals. Grandma set the old cast iron skillet containing a little oil, some seasonings, and the chicken down on the steel grate Grandpa had placed across the cinder blocks of the fireplace. In just a few minutes, the chicken was sizzling merrily away. It soon began to smell good. While Grandma watched the chicken, Grandpa went into the camp to prepare the rest of dinner.

In the woods behind the camp, a passing black bear lifted his nose into the air. His keen sense of smell had discovered the tantalizing aroma of cooking chicken, BBQ sauce, and wood smoke. As a result of his discovery, the bear changed his direction of travel and started to follow the enticing smell that drifted along on the evening breeze. Consequently, he soon found himself coming out of the woods … right behind Grandma Gilbert, who was busily tending to the chicken.

Grandpa Gilbert stepped out of the camp to check on how Grandma was doing with the chicken. He had been in the kitchen preparing corn-on-the-cob and a tossed salad to compliment the BBQ chicken.

"How's the chicken coming, Marjorie?" he asked.

"Just fine Henry," Grandma answered.

As Grandpa turned to go back into the camp, he noticed a movement out of the corner of his eye. Turning to see what it was, he saw the bear coming out of the woods and making its way toward the fireplace and Grandma.

"Marjorie!" he called. "A black bear is coming up behind you, Come in the camp. Hurry!"

Grandma turned and saw the bear, and quickly made her way toward the porch. Then she stopped and looked back.

"Come on, Marjorie. What are you doing?" Grandpa called. Grandma was headed back toward the fireplace and the chicken. "Get in the camp!"

"Not without my chicken," she replied. Still wearing the oven mitt on her hand, she ran back to the fireplace, arriving just seconds before the bear. Grabbing the skillet by the handle, she let out a with a loud, "Shoo!" Then turning quickly, Grandma made a bee-line for the porch. In a second, she was up on the porch and in the camp. Grandpa promptly shut the door.

As a result, the BBQ chicken was safe. The bear, however, was a bit miffed and sniffed around on the porch for several minutes. Finally, the bear figured out that the delicious smelling campfire BBQ chicken was now beyond his reach. The bear reluctantly made his way back into the woods, continuing his search for his supper. No BBQ chicken for him!

The campfire BBQ chicken, corn-on-the-cob, and tossed salad made a wonderful dinner. In addition, the rest of the family got to enjoy hearing the tale of how Grandma rescued the chicken from the hungry black bear many times over the years.

A Trip to the Laundromat

Laundry time is always such a thrill in the Adirondacks. For us, it meant a trip to Raquette Lake Village and the laundromat at the Raquette Lake General Store. As kids, we would hang out in the store or on the village dock or play in the old ice storage sheds (the sheds are long gone now) until Mom and Dad finished with the laundry. It was always an adventure.

There are more "modern" laundromats in Old Forge or Eagle Bay, but there was just something nostalgic about the old Raquette Lake Laundromat. We had been using it for generations. In fact, we had been using it before it had moved to its current location at the General Store. I remember it being located for years over near the now since long-gone ice storage sheds.

This particular laundry adventure involved my sister-in-law, Brenda, who'd gone in to the village to do the week's laundry. Brenda had finished loading the clothes, detergent, and the required number of quarters into the washing machines, and the washers started doing their thing. She decided she'd kill some time looking around in the store for a bit. There were always exciting things to check out. The store still has a real-honest-to-goodness butcher providing fantastic cuts of meat, home-made sausage, etc. I guess I should also mention the store carries the best baked goods in the region, delivered fresh daily from Mary's Bakery in Inlet, about ten minutes away.

At the laundromat, in addition to the door from the sandy parking lot, there was a second doorway that led directly into the general store itself. Brenda was just about to head into the general store when she heard an awful banging sound coming from outside the laundromat. She went to the exterior door to investigate.

It did not take long to determine what was causing the banging noises. Near the laundromat sat the store's dumpster and standing on top of the dumpster was a medium-sized black bear. The bear had a hold of the dumpster lid on which it was standing, and was rearing back, trying to pull it open. Of course, since the bear was also standing on the lid, it would only open so far before the bear's weight slammed it back down with a loud bang!

Brenda quickly went into the general store and over to the counter.

"There's a bear out there on your dumpster, trying to get it open," Brenda exclaimed.

"Oh, that's just Charlie! He won't hurt anything. Charlie makes regular appearances to our dumpster. We wait until he's done before we try to put anything else in it."

Brenda considered this new information carefully for a bit before cautiously returning to check on the laundry. Charlie was still poking around the dumpster but seemed to have little interest in the goings-on in the laundromat. Brenda quickly transferred the clean clothes from the washing machines to some dryers and went back into the store area. When she returned sometime later to check on the dry clothes, Charlie had apparently moved on.

That is what I always love about Raquette Lake! Even the weekly trip to the laundromat can turn into an exciting adventure.

The Bear Trap

Family reunions and joint camping trips to Golden Beach Campground on Raquette Lake were a big tradition for our entire family. Grandparents, aunts, uncles, and cousins all got together in adjoining campsites for a week or two. These are some of my fondest memories growing up. One such particular camping trip also involved a couple of guys from New York City and setting a trap for a mischievous black bear.

My grandfather, Irwin Klippel and his brother, Wagner Klippel, had two campsites that were not quite adjoining. A couple of younger men from New York City occupied the spot separating their two camps sites. The two men had driven up to spend a week in the Adirondack Park. Being very friendly, and since they were camping between two contingents of our family, they just naturally kind of joined the family. They'd brought all the best camping equipment money could buy, as well as a great selection of food including steaks, hot dogs, ground beef and bacon. They were very well prepared for the week

That next morning, the first of their camping experience, the two men arose to discover that a bear had gotten into their icebox. They'd stored their icebox under one end of the park-provided picnic table. The lid was now laying a few feet from the icebox, which was quite empty. The bear ate everything. Everything, that is, except the package of hot dogs, which now lay discarded near the icebox's cover. Someone commented that if the hot dogs weren't good enough for the bear, they weren't eating them either! Anyway, it must have been a hungry (and stealthy) bear. Nobody heard a sound!

After the initial excitement wore off, the two men headed into Indian Lake to restock their supplies. They also decided that it would be better to put their icebox in the trunk of their car when they went to bed at night. While the two men were off getting groceries, we sat around talking about the bear. The focus of the discussion was what could be done to discourage this bear from future raids on our campsites. By the time the men were back from the Grand Union in Indian

Lake, we had devised a plan. The two city guys thought our scheme was a pretty slick idea as well.

That night after supper, we gathered up all the dirty pots and pans from cooking the various family meals and filled them with water. Then we stacked them up, one on top of the other, on the picnic table in the two men's campsite. With several large family units, the supply of dirty cooking pots was indeed adequate for the task at hand. They made quite an impressive, however, slightly unstable tower. My grandmother (the one we called Nanny) made spaghetti in a big metal pot that night. That big pot, with the left-over spaghetti and grease from cooking the ground beef, went on the very top.

In addition, one of the two men parked their car, aiming the headlights at the picnic table. He then tied a length of fishing line to the knob of the light switch on their car's dashboard and strung the fishing line back into the tent. His idea was to turn on the car's headlights by pulling the string when they heard the ruckus the pots and pans would cause. All the kids gathered up flashlights and climbed into vehicles, planning to stay awake and see what happened when the bear came around!

All of a sudden, we heard a loud crashing, bashing sound. All the kids had fallen asleep, but the horrible noise woke everyone up quickly. Several flashlights snapped on and pointed toward the picnic table. The headlights of the car flipped on. And there, right in the beam of the lights, stood a very angry big black bear. He was swaying back and forth with water dripping from him, and with a very perplexed look on his face. There were pots and pans scattered all around him. A few greasy left-over spaghetti noodles hung from one of his ears. The bear let out a bawling kind of grunt and took off running into the trees. The bear trap worked!

My grandfather later told me that he had talked to a park ranger at the campground sometime after that, and the ranger had told him that they did not see that bear in the campground for at least six months after we sprang our trap.

Sophie and the Three Bears

It was a beautiful day. I decided to take Sophie for a good long walk. We left the camp and turned left on Burketown Road. Our camp was near the end of the road which circled to the right, connecting the three parallel tracks that ran from Burke's Marina and Raquette Lake into the area where all the privately-owned camps sat. As you approached the last of these three roads, an old logging road turned off to the left, making its way deep into the dark woods of the Adirondack Park.

I have walked up this road many times while growing up. Sometimes with parents, sometimes with grandparents, and sometimes with cousins. I am sure my brother, Dan, and I walked up the old road many times as well. As kids, we would not wander too far into those woods. They were very wild and rugged, kind of scary. We did not want to get lost. There was an old camper abandoned back in a good way. That was usually as far as we would go.

I do remember once, when I was very young, walking back on that road to an old abandoned ski slope. If I remember correctly, Fred Burke or maybe his father had started to build the ski slope back in the woods before the state created the Adirondack Park, and the ski slope project was abandoned. I have dim memories of a steep hill, the remains of a tow rope and its equipment, and I even think I remember an old building like a simple ski lodge. But it has been a long time.

I thought Sophie and I could walk back and see what remained of that old ski slope. I assumed there would not be much. The north woods have a way of slowly reclaiming anything that is not continually kept up and maintained.

Sophie and I started up the road into the woods. It is damp in the Adirondacks and the old logging road alternated between dark, shaded tracks, muddy patches, and a few open grassy stretches. Raspberry bushes often lined both sides of the old logging road where the sun could reach. Many smaller trees were growing up in the old roadbed. Sophie was having a ball; her nose was always working, checking out all the new and exciting smells. We reached the old abandoned camper and stopped for a short rest. It was then that I noticed

Sophie was acting a little strange. She certainly did not like something.

"Sophie, what's the matter? Come here girl," I called.

Sophie came right up to me. I had taken her leash off once we were in the woods. For some reason, I decided to put her leash back on her at that point. Leashing her turned out to be a good thing. I looked up the road in the direction that led to the old ski slope, and a black bear stepped out onto the track. It stood there motionless, staring at us.

Suddenly there was another movement just off the road to the bear's right. A small black bear cub poked its head up out of some raspberry bushes near the road. Seconds later, a second bear cub's head appeared. Two bear cubs were peering curiously at Sophie and me from behind the raspberry bushes. The mother bear, however, was watching Sophie and me intently, not curiously! I knew this was not a safe place to be. The mother bear "woofed" and began stomping the ground with her front paws. The mother bear "woofing" at us was even worse. It is a warning from the bear! Leave or else!

Sophie was standing stock still, staring fixedly at the mother bear in the road. I was willing her not to bark. I knew her instinct would be to protect me.

"Sophie, easy!" I whispered. "Sophie, come! Come!" I said, still whispering. I began to back up slowly, pulling Sophie with me. She came along but would not take her eyes off the bear. Sophie's ears were at attention. Every muscle in her body was quivering.

We backed slowly down the road in the direction from which we had just come, both of us keeping a very watchful eye on the mother bear. The bear stood watching us but fortunately did not charge. We were leaving.

Once we got around the first bend in the road, we turned, and I led Sophie out of there at a quick pace. Both Sophie and I felt our heartbeats slowly return to a reasonable rate. I decided the old ski slope would have to wait for another day!

About the Author

D.C. Gilbert was born in Ilion, NY but grew up in the Berkshire Mountains of Massachusetts. While growing up, he spent every summer vacation at Raquette Lake in the Adirondack Park of New York State.

An avid reader, he particularly enjoys military history, epic sagas, spy novels, and historical fiction. In addition to serving in the U.S. Army from 1979 to 1983, Darren has over 33 years of martial arts training including managing his own martial arts school for 12 years. He has earned both undergraduate and graduate degrees from the University of Tennessee and Western Governors University respectively. He is also a graduate of Executive Security International's Executive Protection Program and is a Certified Protection Specialist.

Darren currently lives in Cary, NC with his German Shepherd, Sophie.

Author's Note

Did you enjoy reading Adirondack Bear Tales? Reviews are essential to new authors like me. If you did enjoy the story, please take a few minutes to give it a review with the online seller of your choice. Thank you!

DC Gilbert's military action thriller, **Serpents Underfoot**, as well as this collection of short stories, **Adirondack Bear Tales**, are available from Amazon.com.

For more information:
Web: https://darrencgilbert.com
Email: darren@darrencgilbert.com
Instagram: darrencgilbert
Twitter: @darrencgilbert

Made in the USA
Monee, IL
07 December 2020